Do You Like Cooking?

Diane Lindsey Reeves

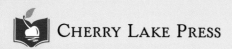

CHERRY LAKE PRESS

Published in the United States of America by Cherry Lake Publishing Group
Ann Arbor, Michigan
www.cherrylakepublishing.com

Reading Adviser: Beth Walker Gambro, MS, Ed., Reading Consultant, Yorkville, IL

Photo Credits: cover: © Anton Chernov/Shutterstock; page 5: © NADKI/Shutterstock; page 6: © Happy Together/ Shutterstock; page 7: © AnnGaysorn/Shutterstock; page 8: © Odua Images/Shutterstock; page 9: © Ikonoklast Fotografie/Shutterstock; page 10: © Monkey Business Images/Shutterstock; page 11: © Rawpixel.com/Shutterstock; page 12: © Drazen Zigic/Shutterstock; page 13: © DC Studio/Shutterstock; page 14: © Jacob Lund/Shutterstock; page 15: © VH-studio/Shutterstock; page 16: © Juice Flair/Shutterstock; page 17: © Juice Verve/Shutterstock; page 18: © DC Studio/Shutterstock; page 19: © JuYochi/Shutterstock; page 20: © Gorodenkoff/Shutterstock; page 21: © Artem Varnitsin/Shutterstock; page 22: USDA's Food and Nutrition Service (FNS); page 23: USDA, Supplemental Nutrition Assistance Program; page 24: © Rido/Shutterstock; page 25: © Monkey Business Images/Shutterstock; page 26: © AYA images/Shutterstock; page 27: © Monkey Business Images/Shutterstock; page 30: © chalermphon_tiam/Shutterstock; page 31: © Eleonora_os/Shutterstock

Cherry Lake Press is an imprint of Cherry Lake Publishing Group.

Library of Congress Cataloging-in-Publication Data has been filed and is available at catalog.loc.gov

Cherry Lake Publishing Group would like to acknowledge the work of the Partnership for 21st Century Learning, a Network of Battelle for Kids. Please visit *http://www.battelleforkids.org/networks/p21* for more information.

Printed in the United States of America
Corporate Graphics

Diane Lindsey Reeves likes to write books that help students figure out what they want to be when they grow up. She mostly lives in Washington, D.C., but spends as much time as she can in North Carolina and South Carolina with her grandkids.

CONTENTS

Cooking Up a Cool Career

Figuring out what you want to be when you grow up can be tricky. There are so many choices! How are you supposed to know which one to pick? Here's an idea... follow the clues!

The fact that you are reading a book called *Do You Like Cooking?* is your first clue. It suggests that you have an interest in food. True? If so, start looking at different ways to cook up a cool career! Your **interests** say a lot about who you are and what makes you tick. What do you like doing best?

Abilities are things that you are naturally good at doing. Another word for ability is talent. Everyone has natural talents and abilities. Some are more obvious than others. What are you really good at doing?

Curiosity offers up other career clues. To succeed in any career, you have to learn what it takes to do that job. You may have to go to college or trade school. It means gaining new skills and getting experience. Curiosity about a subject keeps you at it until you are an expert. What do you want to know more about?

Interests. Abilities. Curiosity. These clues can help you find a career that's right for you.

FIND THE CLUES!

Each chapter includes several clues about careers you might enjoy.

INTERESTS: **What do you like doing?**

ABILITIES: **What are you good at doing?**

CURIOSITY: **What do you want to learn more about?**

Are You a Future Foodie?

WOULD YOU ENJOY...

Baking wedding cakes and other goodies? (see page 8)

Creating special food for special occasions? (see page 10)

Making gourmet meals in a restaurant? (see page 12)

Planning epic parties? (see page 14)

Teaching students how to cook? (see page 16)

Researching the science behind food? (see page 18)

Owning your own food truck? (see page 20)

Helping others get healthy? (see page 22)

Running a favorite restaurant? (see page 24)

Growing food in the middle of a city? (see page 26)

READ ON FOR MORE CLUES ABOUT FOODIE CAREERS!

Baker

A person who makes and sells bread, cakes, and other pastries.

Wake up, sleepyhead! Bakers often get a very early start in the morning. That way, the goodies they bake are fresh for the day. Bakers get lots of on-the-job training watching other bakers. Some work in bakery shops, restaurants, or grocery stores. Others work for companies that produce huge amounts of baked goods. Of course, it's one thing to make a dozen cupcakes for fun. It's another thing to bake hundreds of cupcakes for work! Pastry chefs are another type of baker. They get special training and work in fancy restaurants. This job is guaranteed to make customers smile!

CLUES!

INTEREST: Making yummy treats

ABILITY: Baking bread from scratch

CURIOSITY: Exploring the world's favorite baked goods

INVESTIGATE!

NOW: Make a special cake for a friend's birthday.

LATER: Work in a bakery and attend cooking school.

Caterer

A person who provides food and drink at a social event.

Caterers work with clients to plan special meals for special events. After all, parties are more fun when someone else does the cooking. Many catering companies are run by their owners. That means a caterer must have cooking and business skills. Caterers work with clients to create the perfect menu for each event. Then they work with staff to prepare the food and serve it with style. Tending to all the details is what makes each event a success.

CLUES!

INTEREST: Thumbing through cookbooks

ABILITY: Cooking dinner for your family

CURIOSITY: Creating interesting menus

INVESTIGATE!

NOW: Help your family prepare the meal for a special holiday.

LATER: Attend a culinary academy or restaurant management program.

Chef

A person who is the top cook in a professional kitchen.

Have you ever been at a restaurant and noticed a person in a tall white hat working in the kitchen? The white hat is called a toque. The person is called a chef. It is their job to prepare your meal. If it is a big restaurant, chefs may supervise other cooks who prepare meals for guests. Chefs are highly skilled cooks. The best ones are very creative. They come up with unique menus. They make food look as good as it tastes!

CLUES!

INTEREST: Going out to eat

ABILITY: Being willing to try new foods

CURIOSITY: How to create gourmet meals

INVESTIGATE!

NOW: Sample different types of cuisine—Italian, Chinese, Thai, and more.

LATER: Train at a cooking school or culinary academy.

Event Planner

A person who plans social events like weddings, parties, and fundraisers.

Any big event has about a million moving parts. At least it seems that way! An event planner's job is to manage all of those details for clients. Event planners plan weddings, parties, and other special occasions. Some plan conventions and business meetings. They do what it takes to show the guests a good time. Their to-do list includes everything from making budgets to hiring a band. Choosing locations. Planning menus. Managing staff. It's all in a day's work for an event planner.

CLUES!

INTEREST: Making memories with friends and family

ABILITY: Planning fun parties

CURIOSITY: How to entertain in style

INVESTIGATE!

NOW: Help out at events at your school.

LATER: Earn a college degree in hospitality management.

Family and Consumer Sciences Teacher

A person who teaches students about foods, apparel design, and child development.

Love to cook and want to teach? Family and consumer sciences (FACS) teachers would answer yes and yes! These educators teach practical life skills classes in middle and high schools. These include cooking, nutrition, sewing, and money management. Some also teach classes about childcare. Their goal is to prepare students for successful lives at home and work. Their classrooms are like life laboratories. There is lots of fun hands-on learning!

CLUES!

INTEREST: Learning new things

ABILITY: Teaching people new skills

CURIOSITY: How to succeed in life

INVESTIGATE!

NOW: Get involved in your school's Family Career and Community Leaders of America (FCCLA) club.

LATER: Earn a college degree in family and consumer sciences.

Food Scientist

A person who researches, creates, or improves safe food and food processes.

What career lets you play with your food and eat your experiments? Food science! These scientists put chemistry, biology, and other sciences to work in two major ways. They work to discover new food sources and develop new food products. They also find ways to keep processed foods safe and healthy. Food scientists work for food manufacturers, government agencies, and food test kitchens. Keeping the world fed with wholesome foods is what this job is all about.

CLUES!

INTEREST: Eating healthy foods

ABILITY: Experimenting in the science lab

CURIOSITY: Exploring kitchen science

INVESTIGATE!

NOW: Read the ingredients labels on foods to see what's in them.

LATER: Earn a college degree in food science or agricultural science.

Food Truck Owner

A person who cooks, serves, and sells from a truck equipped with a kitchen.

Food trucks bring good food to hungry people wherever they may be. They pop up at worksites and at community events. Sometimes they add extra fun to wedding receptions and other special events. Food truck owners have two main jobs. One is to make delicious fast food. The other is to manage their food business. Their first big challenge is figuring out a menu that keeps people coming back for more. Finding their food fans is their best bet for success.

CLUES!

INTEREST: Fresh, fast foods

ABILITY: Cooking new recipes for friends

CURIOSITY: How to run a fun food business

INVESTIGATE!

NOW: Be on the lookout for local food truck rodeos.

LATER: Get experience working in a restaurant.

Nutritionist

A person who helps people develop healthy eating habits.

Nutritionists help people eat their way to good health. Some nutritionists work in schools where they plan meals for students. Their biggest challenge is serving healthy foods that kids will actually eat. Others work in hospitals and nursing homes. Nutrition plays a big part in getting and keeping these patients healthy. Some work with people or sport teams where fitness is the number one goal. Nutritionists set up meal plans and teach patients about health risks. They encourage people to make good food choices. Their message is simple: You are what you eat!

CLUES!

INTEREST: **Good health**

ABILITY: **Choosing food that keeps your body healthy**

CURIOSITY: **How nutrition works**

INVESTIGATE!

NOW: **Learn about two new good food habits and work them into your routine.**

LATER: **Earn a college degree in nutrition and wellness.**

Restaurant Manager

A person who makes sure a restaurant runs smoothly.

When people go out to eat, they expect good food and good service. It is a restaurant manager's job to make sure they get both. Restaurant managers hire and train staff. They also order food and welcome guests. They make sure the restaurant stays clean and meets all safety rules. Many managers get their start as a server or cook. It certainly helps to have good people skills. Hungry people can get grumpy. Keeping staff and customers happy is what they do best.

CLUES!

INTERESTS: Eating out

ABILITIES: Being a team player

CURIOSITY: How restaurants work

INVESTIGATE!

NOW: Try out a new type of restaurant.

LATER: Get training in hospitality or restaurant management.

Urban Farmer

A person who raises animals or produce for food in a city environment.

Once upon a time, farmers lived on farms with acres of land for crops and animals. Some farmers still do. But a growing number of farmers produce food closer to where people live. They look for ways to grow more food in less space. That's where things get really creative. Some can transform an empty lot into a green paradise. Some plant gardens on skyscraper rooftops. Some use hydroponics to plant vertical gardens. That is where rows of plants grow up instead of spreading out. This type of farming brings fresh produce to food deserts. These places lack easy access to grocery stores.

CLUES!

INTERESTS: Farm-to-table foods

ABILITIES: Being a creative problem-solver

CURIOSITY: Smart ways to grow food

INVESTIGATE!

NOW: Try growing a favorite vegetable or fruit.

LATER: Check out training options through a university agricultural extension program.

Cooking Workshop

Keep investigating those career clues until you find a career that's right for you! Here are more ways to explore.

Join a Club

Family Career and Community Leaders of America and 4-H (https://fcclainc.org and https://4-h.org) clubs offer fun opportunities to learn and compete with other foodies.

Talk to People with Interesting Careers

Ask your teacher or parent to help you connect with someone who has a career like the one you want. Be ready to ask lots of questions!

Volunteer

Look for opportunities to help prepare and serve food in your community. Ideas include soup kitchens, school sporting events, and celebrations at your place of worship. Be sure to have permission from your parents or guardian to participate.

Enjoy Career Day

School career days can be a great way to find out more about different careers. Make the most of this opportunity.

Explore Online

With adult supervision, use your favorite search engine to look online for information about careers you are interested in.

Participate in Take Your Daughters and Sons to Work Day

Every year on the fourth Thursday of April, kids all over the world go to work with their parents or other trusted adults. They spend the day finding out what the world of work is really like.

Find out more at: https://daughtersandsonstowork.org

Resources

Baker
Cup Cake Jones: How Many Cupcakes Does a Bakery Make
https://cupcakejones.net/how-many-cupcakes-does-a-bakery-make-per-day

Caterer
The Complete Cookbook for Young Chefs
America's Test Kitchen. *The Complete Cookbook for Young Chefs.* Napierville, IL: Sourcebooks Jabberwocky, 2018.

Chef
Master Chef Junior
https://www.fox.com/masterchef-junior

Event Planner
Planning Perfect Parties
Jones, Jen. *Planning Perfect Parties.* North Mankato, MN: Capstone Press, 2014.

Family and Consumer Studies Teacher
Family, Career and Community Leaders of America (FCCLA)
https://fcclainc.org

Food Scientist
IFT: Careers in Food Science
*https://www.iftevent.org/ift/home/career-development/
learn-about-food-science/careers-in-food-science*

Food Truck Owner
Food Network: America's 26 Best Food Trucks
*https://www.foodnetwork.com/restaurants/photos/best-
food-trucks-in-the-country*

Nutritionist
USDA: My Plate for Kids
https://www.myplate.gov/life-stages/kids

Restaurant Manager
Working in a Restaurant: Everything You Need to Know
https://www.7shifts.com/blog/working-in-a-restaurant

Urban Farmer
California Academy of Sciences: Urban Farming
https://www.calacademy.org/educators/urban-farming

Glossary

abilities (uh-BIH-luh-teez) natural talent or acquired skill to do something

curiosity (kyur-ee-AH-suh-tee) strong desire to know or learn about something

food desert (FOOD DEH-zuhrt) place without easy access to grocery stories

food truck rodeo (FOOD TRUK ROH-dee-oh) event where a group of food trucks gather in one location

gourmet (GOOR-may) high quality food

hydroponics (hye-druh-PAH-niks) growing plants without soil by using water-based mineral nutrient solutions

interests (IN-tuh-ruhsts) things or activities that a person enjoys or is concerned about

menu (MEHN-yoo) list of the dishes or kinds of food served at a meal

processed foods (PRAH-sest FOODZ) foods that have been altered in some way during preparation

toque (TOOK) tall white hat worn by a chef

Index